Date: 10/5/15

J BIO DOUGLAS
Anderson, Jameson,
Gabby Douglas /

TABLE OF CONTENTS

OLYMPIC STAR

It was the 2012 Summer Olympics in London, England. Gabby Douglas was in the lead in the women's gymnastics **all-around** competition.

There are four events in the all-around. Douglas had wowed the crowd in the first three. After competing on the vault, uneven bars, and balance beam, she still kept the lead. During her floor exercise **routine**, Douglas tumbled and twirled across the mat. The world followed along on television.

After her routine, Douglas waited for her results in London's 02 Arena. When her score of 62.232 was displayed, Douglas was in shock. She didn't know how to react until her coach explained it to her. She had won!

Douglas had become just the fourth US Olympic gymnast to earn the all-around gold medal. Plus, she and her fellow US Olympic gymnasts had taken gold as a team just two nights earlier. At 16 years old, Douglas was on top of the podium and at the top of her profession.

Douglas was the first gymnast in US Olympic history to win gold in both the individual all-around and team events!

HIGHLIGHT REEL

Gabrielle Christina Victoria Douglas was born in Virginia Beach, Virginia.

1995

Douglas moved to Iowa to train with coach Liang Chow.

2010

In June, Douglas won gold at the Olympic Trials. She was named to the US Olympic team.

2012

Douglas began training for the 2016 Olympics. They will be held in Rio de Janeiro, Brazil.

2013

2004

Douglas was named Virginia's State Gymnastics Champion.

2011

Douglas helped her team win a gold medal at the World Championships in Tokyo, Japan.

2012

In August, Douglas won two gold medals at the Summer Olympics in London, England.

GABBY DOUGLAS

DOB: December 31, 1995
Ht: 4'11"
Wt: 90
Events: Balance beam, floor exercise, uneven bars, vault
Favorite Events: Balance beam and floor exercise

CAREER STATISTICS:
Olympic Medals: . . . . 2 gold

AWARDS:
Associated Press Female Athlete of the Year: 2012
Olympic team and all-around gold medalist: 2012
Teen Choice Award for Female Athlete: 2013
World Championships team gold medalist: 2011

DIFFICULT START

Gabrielle Christina Victoria "Gabby" Douglas was born on December 31, 1995, in Virginia Beach, Virginia. Her parents are Natalie Hawkins and Timothy Douglas. Gabby's father wasn't around much when she was young. She was raised mostly by her mother and her older **siblings**, Arielle, Joyelle, and Johnathan.

Gabby's early life was difficult. Not long after she was born, doctors discovered that Gabby had a rare blood **disorder**. She suffered from branched chain ketoaciduria. The disorder made it hard for Gabby's body to take in enough **protein**.

Eating was difficult for Gabby when she was an infant. Because of this, she was very small. Eventually, she outgrew the disorder. By six months old, Gabby was able to eat comfortably. She began to gain weight and become healthy.

Gabby is the youngest of four children in her family. Her brother and sisters enjoy attending her events.

FIRST LESSONS

When Gabby was two years old, her sister Arielle was taking gymnastics lessons. Arielle tried to teach her little sister everything she knew. Gabby began tumbling and trying cartwheels at a very young age.

But, Gabby didn't start taking gymnastics lessons until she was six. Gabby's mother worried she might get hurt before that. Arielle helped convince their mother that it was okay.

It didn't take long for Gabby to **excel** at gymnastics. Soon, she was winning competitions at her local gym in Virginia Beach. In 2004, she was named Virginia's State Gymnastics Champion. Gabby scored 38.350. She beat Catalina Palma, who placed second, by less than a point.

In 2008, Gabby competed at the National Junior Championships at the US Classic in Houston, Texas. It was her first time in front of a national audience. Gabby placed tenth in the **all-around**. She scored well enough to move on to the Visa Championships in Boston, Massachusetts.

There, Gabby placed sixteenth with a score of 108.900. The score wasn't high enough for her to make the 2008 Junior Women's National Team. Then, a wrist injury kept Gabby out of competition for most of 2009.

Gabby did gymnastics routines in her living room when she was just four years old. Her flips off the furniture led to her success at gymnastics competitions.

MOVING AWAY

Gabby finally competed in an international meet in September 2010. At the Pan American Championships in Guadalajara, Mexico, Gabby earned a first-place team medal. She won fifth in the **all-around**. Her future Olympic teammate Kyla Ross took first.

It soon became clear to Gabby that she had outgrown the gym where she trained. If she wanted to improve at gymnastics, she needed a new gym and new coaches.

Gabby was also teased at her gym. She was the only African-American gymnast training there. Sometimes, Gabby felt like quitting the sport because some of the other gymnasts were mean to her. Instead, she decided to focus even more on gymnastics.

Still, the decision to leave wasn't up to Gabby alone. As the youngest child in her family, she worried her mother would not let her move. But Natalie said yes!

In 2010, Gabby moved away from her family and friends. She left Virginia Beach for West Des Moines, Iowa. Gabby would train with one of the nation's best gymnastics coaches, Liang Chow.

Gabby moved away from her family when she was just 14 years old. She was excited to work with Coach Chow.

A SECOND FAMILY

Iowa differed from Douglas's home in Virginia Beach. In Iowa, Douglas spent most of her time practicing gymnastics. To make time for training and travel, she was **homeschooled** as she had been in Virginia.

In Iowa, Douglas learned alongside other Olympic hopefuls and world-class gymnasts. Coach Chow had already helped gymnast Shawn Johnson win a silver medal at the 2008 Olympics. He was sure he could coach Douglas to success at the next Olympic Games in 2012.

When she wasn't at the gym, Douglas was with her host family. Travis and Missy Parton welcomed her into their home. They watched out for her while she was away from her mother. The Parton family has four girls, all younger than Douglas.

Douglas was shy at first with the Partons. It wasn't easy for her to ask for things from them. In time, Douglas became more comfortable with the Partons. She now refers to them as her "second family."

Missy Parton, Natalie Hawkins, and retired Olympic medalist Shawn Johnson (*left to right*)

THE ROAD TO GOLD

Douglas's journey to the Olympics was achieved through a lot of practice. She had to keep winning smaller competitions so people would see her talent. Starting in 2010, she rose up through the competition. Douglas earned the attention of the US National Team and the world's gymnastics fans.

In 2010, she won gold on the uneven bars at the Pan American Championships. And, she won silver at the US Junior National Championships on the balance beam. She scored 28.550. Kyla Ross beat her with a score of 29.900. Ross was later named the US Junior National **all-around** champion.

On October 11, 2011, Douglas competed at the World Championships in Tokyo, Japan. For the team competition, she competed on the uneven bars. And with her help, the team won a gold medal!

At just 15 years old, Douglas was not only the youngest US competitor at the World Championships in Tokyo. She was the youngest gymnast at the entire event!

At the event, just two athletes from each country could go on to compete for the individual **all-around**. Douglas ranked fifth overall, but two of her teammates ranked above her. So, she was not able to compete for another medal. Still, Douglas's success was impressive.

On June 10, 2012, Douglas competed at the Visa Championships in St. Louis, Missouri. The event helped determine which gymnasts would go to the Olympic Trials later that month.

Douglas finished second in the overall championship after Jordyn Wieber. After facing each other so often, the two had become friends. The strong competition between them helped them practice harder and improve. Both moved on to the Olympic Trials in San Jose, California.

On June 29, 2012, Douglas's Olympic dream came true. The top-performing girls at the trials were named to the official US Olympic team. Douglas won the entire Olympic Trials competition. She had the only guaranteed spot on the Olympic team. She was headed to London!

The Olympic Trials were also special to Douglas for another reason. She was able to see her father for the first time in two years. Timothy Douglas had served in the US Air Force in Afghanistan. He returned to surprise Douglas at the competition.

Douglas, along with McKayla Maroney, Jordyn Wieber, Kyla Ross, and Aly Raisman (*left to right*), were named to the US Olympic team. Together, the girls would be known at the Olympics as the Fierce Five.

THE FLYING SQUIRREL

Even before the Olympics, Douglas competed in international events as part of the US team. But in individual events, her teammates were also her competitors. This included Kyla Ross. Douglas had also faced Jordyn Wieber many times at tournaments.

Most gymnasts have a favorite event. Douglas and Wieber are both known for their floor **routines**. Douglas also loves the balance beam. But she is known for how high she flies on the uneven bars. In fact, she is called "The Flying Squirrel." US Nationals Team Coordinator Martha Karolyi gave her the nickname in 2011.

More people learned her nickname during the Olympics. The **unique** name was the subject of many interview questions. A lot of reporters asked Douglas if she minded having the nickname of a **rodent**. Douglas said she didn't mind. She said squirrels are cute and adventurous!

The Flying Squirrel enjoys reaching new heights when she performs on the uneven bars. She loves to make the crowd gasp!

RECORD SETTER

At the 2012 Olympics, Douglas set many milestones for female gymnasts, especially African-American gymnasts. On August 2, she became the first gymnast of African descent in Olympic history to become the Individual **All-Around** Champion.

Douglas scored 15.966 on the vault and 15.733 on the uneven bars. She earned 15.500 on the balance beam and 15.033 in the floor exercise, for a total of 62.232. Douglas won by less than one point over Viktoria Komova of Russia.

Douglas also became the first American gymnast to win gold in both the individual all-around and team competitions at the same Olympics. Douglas and the "Fierce Five" team won the team all-around gold medal on July 31. They scored 183.596. This was more than five points higher than silver medalists Russia.

DOMINIQUE DAWES

DOUGLAS WAS INSPIRED BY DOMINIQUE DAWES. IN 1996, DAWES WAS THE FIRST AFRICAN-AMERICAN GYMNAST TO WIN AN OLYMPIC MEDAL. SHE AND DOUGLAS MET AFTER THE 2012 OLYMPICS. DOUGLAS SAID SHE WAS FLATTERED THAT SO MANY PEOPLE HAD COMPARED HER TO DAWES.

During practice, Coach Chow asked his gymnasts to gather around the balance beam and cheer Douglas on as she performed her routines. This helped her learn how to focus and block out the audience's cheers at the Olympics.

Douglas didn't do as well in other individual events. The Flying Squirrel finished eighth on the uneven bars. This was the lowest score of any of the eight gymnasts who qualified for the finals in the event. Her score was 14.900. In the balance beam finals, Douglas finished in seventh place with a score of 13.633.

OLYMPIC FAME

Since her Olympic wins, Douglas has become one of the most recognizable US athletes. Many companies have wanted Douglas to do advertisements for them. She has appeared in commercials for Nike, AT&T, and Nintendo.

Douglas's popularity has also landed her on television shows. In 2012, she appeared on the Disney TV series *Kickin' It!* and the show *The Vampire Diaries*. She also served as a guest judge on the popular competition show *So You Think You Can Dance*.

Douglas has appeared on many talk shows, including news and health cooking shows. Awards shows such as the 2012 MTV Video Music Awards and the 2013 Nickelodeon Kids' Choice Awards have also featured Douglas.

Douglas was featured on a box of Corn Flakes cereal with her Olympic medals.

In February 2014, *The Gabby Douglas Story* was released on Lifetime Television. Douglas and her mother were **producers** of the movie, which told Douglas's life story. As producers, they were able to tell the story they wanted to tell.

Actress Imani Hakim played Douglas in the movie. However, Douglas did **stunt** work for the movie. When Hakim could not do the gymnastics moves required for a scene, Douglas performed them. The movie also featured film of some of Douglas's Olympic performances.

Between training, studying, and celebrity appearances, Douglas found time to write books. She released two books after her Olympic wins. The first book is an **autobiography** titled *Grace, Gold & Glory: My Leap of Faith*. It was published in December 2012.

In the book, Douglas tells her life story. She wants to help inspire other girls to live their dreams. She encourages them to be the best at what they do.

In May 2013, Douglas released a second book. This book, titled *Raising the Bar*, is a more lighthearted look at Douglas's life. Douglas shares things about her family and friends, her favorite foods, and even her training **routines**.

Douglas enjoys talking with fans and signing autographs.

NEXT OLYMPICS

After the media attention settled down, Douglas took some time off from gymnastics. She wanted to spend more time with her family. They had moved from Virginia Beach to Los Angeles, California. Douglas moved with them.

In Los Angeles, Douglas began to train on her own. Her goal was to return to the US Championships. She focused on the 2016 Olympics, which will be held in Rio de Janeiro, Brazil. For that, Douglas will train again with Coach Chow in Iowa.

At the 2016 Olympics, Douglas will compete as one of the world's greatest gymnasts and popular athletes. Fans from around the world will be cheering for her. They are hoping to see her repeat as overall champion.

GIVING BACK

IN 2016, THE NATIONAL MUSEUM OF AFRICAN AMERICAN HISTORY AND CULTURE WILL OPEN AT THE SMITHSONIAN INSTITUTION IN WASHINGTON, DC. DOUGLAS DONATED SOME PERSONAL ITEMS FOR THE MUSEUM'S EXHIBITS. THESE INCLUDE THE LEOTARD FROM HER FIRST COMPETITIVE SEASON, PERSONAL PHOTOS, UNEVEN BAR GRIPS FROM THE OLYMPICS, AND HER MOTHER'S TICKET TO THE GAMES.

Douglas competes on the balance beam in the individual all-around event at the 2012 Olympics.

GLOSSARY

all-around - involving performances on every apparatus used in a competition.

autobiography - a story of a person's life that is written by himself or herself.

disorder - a physical or mental condition that is not normal or healthy.

excel - to be better than others.

homeschool - to teach children at home rather than in a traditional school setting.

producer - a person who oversees or provides money for a play, television show, movie, or album.

protein - a substance which provides energy to the body and serves as a major class of foods for animals. Foods high in protein include cheese, eggs, fish, meat, and milk.

rodent - any of several related animals that have large front teeth for gnawing. Common rodents include mice, squirrels, and beavers.

routine (roo-TEEN) - a group of actions that are repeated as part of a performance.

sibling - a brother or a sister.

stunt - an action requiring great skill or daring.

unique (yoo-NEEK) - being the only one of its kind.

To learn more about Awesome Athletes, visit **booklinks.abdopublishing.com**. These links are routinely monitored and updated to provide the most current information available.

INDEX